IN

CANOE AND CAMERA

A

TWO-HUNDRED MILE TOUR

THROUGH

THE MAINE FORESTS

Thomas Sedgwick Steele gives us a story of what it was like in 1879 to travel through the Maine woods. In actuality, if you took this trip today most of the miles would reveal themselves to look the same as seen by Steele. In fact, in some instances, with the disappearance of logging camps and supply depots, the route is more remote than it was during his time. Since then, the Allagash Wilderness Waterway has been designated and this part of Maine will remain forever wild.

.

A

Burnt Jacket Publishing

Classic Release

CANOE AND CAMERA

A

TWO HUNDRED MILE TOUR

THROUGH

THE MAINE FORESTS

–

Annotated Edition

BY

THOMAS SEDGWICK STEELE

Updated by

TOMMY CARBONE, PH.D.

MOUNT KINEO - 2020

"If thou art worn and hard beset

With sorrows that thou wouldst forget,

If thou wouldst read a lesson, that will keep

Thy heart from fainting, and thy soul from sleep,

Go to the woods and hills! — no tears

Dim. the sweet look that Nature wears."

Henry Wadsworth Longfellow

With Illustrations.

NEW YORK

ORANGE JUDD COMPANY

245 BROADWAY

1880.

CANOE AND CAMERA
ANNOTATED EDITION

Cover photos, and new interior photographs from the
collection of Tommy Carbone or as otherwise noted.
Cover design by Tommy Carbone.
Newly added material and editing by Tommy Carbone.

Use of newly added copyrighted material (text and photos)
from this book, other than short passages for review purposes
or used within quotations, requires prior written permission be
obtained by contacting the publisher at
info@tommycarbone.com.

Burnt Jacket Publishing

Greenville, Maine

20210326 AMPB

ISBN: 978-1-954048-03-4

Also available in Commemorative Hardcover Edition

www.tommycarbone.com

UPDATED EDITION

TABLE OF CONTENTS

THE SPENCER MOUNTAINS - 2020

Introduction – Updated Edition

*

On discovering there was a book by Thomas Sedgwick Steele about the Maine North Woods, I set out to find a copy. After searching, I was disappointed in the copies that were available. Either they were old and falling apart, or they were republished without regard for the historical importance of this work. It was then I decided to expend the effort, for what most surely will be a small monetary return, but for what I trust will give those few readers who discover this volume a great deal of satisfaction.

There are many explorers that still visit the part of the Maine woods Steele describes. Some visit for a day, while others spend weeks paddling and hiking the back-country. This book is a perfect companion for a journey through some of the most pristine wilderness in America, whether you go in person, or from the comfort of your favorite chair.

Enjoy the story.

Tommy Carbone, Ph.D.

2020 Edition Editor of, *"Canoe and Camera."*
Greenville, Maine
October, 2020

www.tommycarbone.com

THE AUTHOR'S SANCTUM

about

THOMAS SEDGWICK STEEL

(1845 – 1903)

2020 Edition

Thomas Sedgwick Steel was a writer, a photographer, an illustrator, and an avid American outdoorsman. He was born in Hartford, Connecticut and started out in his father's jewelry business. In 1880, he published the book you hold, "Canoe and Camera." Not only was his writing descriptive of the adventures he had, but he included illustrated engravings, many of which were from his own paintings.

Along with his writing and paintings, he also issued a map of northern Maine. An image of Steele's map has been included in this edition.

ORIGINAL DEDICATION

Typed Dedication

To my enthusiastic friends of the gun and rod,
who love all that is pure and beautiful in nature,
and by associating with her works, learn of
man's littleness in comparison with God's
immensity, this book is affectionately dedicated.

Thomas Sedgwick Steele

Hartford Conn. 1880

CANOE AND CAMERA

Detailed Contents

List of Illustrations

Annotated Edition Photographs

1880 Introduction

A LOVE for the woods and out-door sports begins early in life. I can hardly remember when the sight of a gun or fish-rod did not awaken within my boyish fancy a feverish desire to follow their lead, be the tramp ever so hard. There never was anything to stop the growth of this passion until I reached the age of ten years, when I nearly destroyed a boy's eye with an arrow, in my endeavors to excel in archery.

This act slightly dampened my ardor for some months, and retarded that progression in field sports I was then making.

There is also something so free, so stimulating in the woods life, uncontaminated by the gossip, allurements, and exacting dress of the usual watering places, that after one season's enjoyment, a return to these wildernesses, and repeating its pleasures, is the constant thought of the future.

> *"Man's rich with little, were his judgment true;*
>
> *Nature is frugal, and her wants are few."*

It also teaches very early self-reliance, and a philosophical endurance of many conditions of life, which add to one's cheerfulness, while one is surprised how few of the necessities are essential to produce happiness.

The study also of natural history in the woods takes one into a realm which has no bounds, constantly enlarging his love and admiration of God's works. The oft-repeated quotation, "Spare the rod and spoil the child," has been misconstrued for many a long day, and if I had known early in life its real significance it would hardly have made so doleful an impression.

There is no doubt today in my mind that this "rod" meant a fishing-rod, and that the timely cherishing of it in youth tends to develop that portion of one's nature to which the former use was entirely innocent.

"The surest road to health, say what you will,

Is never to suppose we shall be ill.

Most of those evils we poor mortals know

From doctors and imagination flow."

And now, after spending many of the annual short vacations allotted to an active business life in various parts of this country, from Canada to Florida, in the exhilarating sport of hunting, fishing, and exploring, and deriving great physical good thereby, it would not seem strange that the writer should be desirous of exciting in the hearts of others a taste for like recreations. In placing before my readers this sketch of a late canoe tour through Maine — especially that portion pertaining to the east branch of the Penobscot — I am perfectly aware that no two trips through that region can be made under the same circumstances. All days in the woods are alike, and still they are very unlike. Weather, height of water, companions, canoes, guides, sunshine or shadow, a hundred and one things, go to make a day pleasant or unpleasant to the tourist. During the month occupied in making this trip, the writer experienced but *four* days of rain. But the first rain-storm could not have been more opportune, as it raised the water of Webster Stream to a height that permitted the passage of my four canoes, when otherwise I should have endured a wearisome "carry" of seven miles. Unless there is sufficient water in Webster stream to float a canoe with *ease,* I should not recommend the tour of the East Branch, for the numerous portages will hardly compensate for the pleasures of the trip.

The writer distinctly remembers meeting an angler who had followed the recommendation of a guide book on Maine, and attempted the journey from Allagash river to Chamberlin Lake. Instead of an abundance of water, the stream was almost dry, and a "carry" of seven miles had to be made to Chamberlin Lake. Again, the canvas boat added no little enjoyment to the pleasures of the excursion, and the trip would have lost many of its bright experiences without its companionship.

True, it received many a cut, but was more easily repaired than a birch bark, while its qualities of endurance after such an ordeal permitted it to spend the following winter season under the tropical skies of Florida.

No better companion could have been selected than Mr. H. R. Morley, of the Continental Life Insurance Company, Hartford (the "quartermaster" of the expedition), and to his suggestions and efforts to make the best of all difficulties the writer acknowledges himself indebted. It is surprising how selfishness, egotism, and other like traits of character will develop in the woods when it was never recognized in the individual at home, and one must have the true spirit of patient endurance for the sake of accomplishment in order at times to enjoy the forest life.

Thus, the entire trip was made on the "flood tide," from the state of the weather to the volume of water in the streams, facilitating the taking of photographs, and adding height and power to the many picturesque falls on the route. Until I am corrected by further explorations, I think I am right in the discovery of a new lake (not found on any map), between Matagamonsis and Matagamon lakes.

An enlargement of Hay Creek has been suggested as this body of water, but if so, all the larger lakes in this region are but a part of the preceding stream which empties into them. This lake has the same area of square miles as Telosmis Lake, and empties its waters into the sluggish stream which connects the two large bodies of water just mentioned.

The pleasure of canoeing these undiscovered lakes and streams, and living from day to day upon their resources, was an element of indescribable delight. Nowhere do such rich thoughts of God's bounty, grandeur, and control of nature impress one as in the depths of the forests, and there are reveries forced upon one, for which a city of brick walls and dusty streets have no affinity. The individuality of each tree, the strange and rare plants and flowers scattered along the indistinct path one wanders, all coupled with the weird stillness of the forest, bring one nearer to God and His works than almost any other situation. I do not suggest in this book the various ways of camping out, or the necessary preparations for the same, as there are special works on those subjects; I simply desire to direct the attention of tourists, and more especially artists, to a section of Maine *now but little known*, but which, if once explored, will yield to them a bright harvest of pleasure and studies.

THE AUTHOR.   HARTFORD, CONN.

READY TO GO

(Editor's Collection)

CANOE AND CAMERA

A

TWO HUNDRED MILE TOUR

THROUGH

THE MAINE FORESTS

ILLUSTRATED
BY
True Williams, Benjamin Day, Aug. Will,
And Other Artists.

Chapter I

*

"I in these flowery meads would be;
These crystal streams should solace me;
To whose harmonious, bubbling noise
I with my angle would rejoice."

WALTON.

AN ANGLER'S SOLILOQUY. — ISAAK WALTON'S
IDEAS. — A FISHING MINISTER. — THE ROUTE TO
THE WOODS. — MOOSEHEAD LAKE AND
VICINITY.

*

IN the good old times, when the requirements of business kept one out in the open air, and each client or patient resided many miles away, and the only communication was by foot or on horseback, one did not need the indispensable rest and recreation of today.

But now all is changed, and within a hand's grasp at our offices we can communicate by the strange wires of the telephone or telegraph with friends miles away, and save ourselves those steps which would no doubt be of great benefit if taken.[1]

---

[1] **2020:** Consider Steele's words from 1880 against today's speed and connectivity of the internet and smartphones.

In this fast world of ours, where the work of a week is crowded into a day, recreation is a necessity, and nowhere, it seems to me, has it greater recuperative power than in the depths of the forest.

It is not as a plea for the angler that I pen these lines — he asks for neither judge nor jury on his tastes, although they no doubt frequently receive the verdict of both; he is a law unto himself.

"It is a very easy thing to scoff at any art or recreation, a little wit mixed with ill-nature, confidence, and malice will do it, though they are often caught in their own trap."

It is only a few weeks since that I was rallied on my pet hobby by a prominent business man, who thought one could hardly be in his right mind who had a fondness for life in the woods, and that it must give one a tendency to coarseness, rather than improving our higher and more esthetic tastes. But this gentleman was welcome to his ideas, for he was then an invalid from a nervous disease, and had spent the prime of his life regaining his health, when possibly an occasional day's tramp beside a trout stream would have been a matter of economy to both purse and body.

The father of anglers, Isaak Walton,[2] puts this same idea in a still better light, for although born in 1593, he knew how

---

[2] **2020**: Walton first published, *The Compleat Angler* in 1653. The chapters on fly fishing and flies were expanded by Charles Cotton in the 1676 fifth edition of the book.

to read the human nature of today; he says: "Yes! there are many grave and serious men who pity us anglers, but there are many more grave and serious men whom we anglers condemn and pity."

"Men that are taken to be grave because nature hath made them of a sour complexion, money getting men that spend all their time, first in getting, and next in anxious care to keep it! Men that are condemned to be rich, and then always busy and discontented — for these poor rich men we anglers pity them perfectly, and stand in no need to borrow their thoughts to think ourselves so happy."

ISAAK WALTON

Someone has said that an angler consists of a rod with a fool at one end and a fish at the other. But Walton, in his meanderings beside the streams, is reported to have had the constant companionship of a book, and between the nibbles of the fish stored his mind with useful knowledge.

While hunting in the western part of Connecticut last autumn, a good story was told me of a minister who, soon after his settlement in the parish, greatly annoyed his flock by his habitual fondness for angling. He would start off early on Monday morning, and would keep up the diversion until late Saturday night; nevertheless, the quality of his sermons, and the deep thoughts which they contained, so pleased his people that similar excursions were suggested to the pastors of other churches in the town.

So much for an introduction to the inmost thoughts of a lover of the angle, but possibly you would like to know how to reach the solitudes of Maine, whose influences are so bewitching to the writer, and where, with the reader as companion, he proposes to enjoy a canoe ride of two hundred miles.

To one about to make a trip to Maine, we would say, start in all cases from Boston, even though you live in Chicago. Take the 7 P. M. express on the Eastern railroad for Bangor, thereby having a good night's rest in a sleeper, awaking refreshed for the pleasures of the next day's journey.

But those who have never traveled this road will do well to see their flight be not in the night, for, commencing with Boston, its main line extends along the shore, giving here and there glimpses of quiet bays and shady inlets, and through cities noted for their thrift and prosperity almost from the country's settlement.

One would be well repaid for a day spent at almost any station along the route, as the eastern shore of New England has often been the subject for busy pens and famous pencils. From Massachusetts Bay to Passamaquoddy and the Isle of Great Manan,[3] it is filled with nooks and beaches where, in the hot months of summer, the seeker for rest and renewed health can choose the spot suited to his taste. The Eastern railroad — with its numerous branches and connecting lines — forms the most direct and desirable means of access to these points of interest.

It does not, however, limit the choice to the seashore, for it leads also to the heart of the famous White Mountains, and to the vast and partially explored lake region of Maine, towards which I had set my face.

Lynn, eleven miles from Boston, famed for its immense factories of boots and shoes, lies at the head of Nahant Bay, from which there is a delightful drive along the shore to Nahant, a noted, picturesque watering place. Nearby is

---

[3] **2020**: Grand Manan, the Canadian island in the Bay of Fundy, New Brunswick.

Swampscott, its shores lined with summer cottages, and from here a short branch road runs to rocky Marblehead, a spot mentioned in letters of travel as early as the year 1633.

Salem, four miles further on, famous since the days of witchcraft, and once the principal port of entry for New England, not only has its pleasant situation to attract the visitor, but is full of relics of the olden time of interest to the antiquary. It was the birthplace of many men whose names have become a part of our nation's history and literature.

At Beverly, the Gloucester branch leads down to the sea at Cape Ann, with its sunny beaches and rocky head lands, quiet when the wind is off shore, but where the waves come thundering in when driven before an easterly gale.

But we have hardly time to speak of Newburyport, another old seacoast town, and the lovely view to be had from its heights of the surrounding country and ocean, but hasten through to Salisbury, Hampton, and Rye Beach.

Portsmouth is quiet and quaint, and at Conway Junction, eleven miles from Portsmouth, passengers change cars for the White Mountains. At Portland, the angler makes choice of the routes to the two great trouting paradises of Maine — Rangeley Lakes and Moosehead Lake.

KINEO HOUSE,

THE KINEO HOUSE

If to the former place, he takes the cars for Farmington, eighty-five miles directly north from Portland, and then by stage thirty-six miles over the mountains to Kimball's Head of the First Rangeley Lake, where he will receive a hearty welcome from as cordial a company of fishermen as it has been my pleasure in other seasons to enjoy.

If the latter be his choice, guns, rods, blankets, and other camp equipage are shifted to the train of the Maine Central railroad for Bangor, where the cars are again changed for the road to Blanchard, which is twelve miles from Moosehead Lake. After a substantial dinner, the tourist mounts to the top of the commodious Concord stage drawn by four horses, and enjoys a delightful ride of eleven miles over the hills to Greenville, foot of Moosehead Lake. Here the baggage is again changed to a steamer, and a most enjoyable sail of twenty miles lands one at the Kineo House, which stands on a prominent point of rocks extending far out into Moosehead Lake, a convenient center of attraction for those who dislike the unadulterated life in the woods.

Annotated Edition

The Kineo House was a grand hotel on the peninsula that stretches out midway up the lake from which rises Mt. Kineo. The resort had its start in the 1840s when a tavern was first opened, and it quickly became a frequent spot for hunters and fishermen.

Over the years the Mount Kineo house was built and rebuilt at least three times. The first was built in 1848 and was in operation until it burned in 1868.

The rebuilt property opened in 1871 and was expanded until it too was destroyed by fire in 1882.

In 1884 a new Mount Kineo House opened with a dining hall that accommodated over 400 guests, a golf course, a music room, and a billiard hall.

In 1911 the Central Maine Railroad purchased the property. By the 1930s the grand hotel started to see a marked decrease in occupancy. With the invention and affordability of the automobile, tourists were less dependent on railways to take them to their destination. In

1938 the government, as part of an antitrust case, discontinued subsidies for mail-carrying railroads that owned other businesses. The Central Maine Railroad cited dwindling ridership and sold the property.

Today, visitors reach the peninsula by ferry from Rockwood or by private boat. Once there, you can play nine holes on the golf course or hike one of several trails to the top of Mt. Kineo.

Many travelers in the 1800s and early 1900s began their north woods excursion with a stop at the Kineo House before departing for the northwest or northeast carries.

Steamers would transport parties to the northern most portion of the lake. From there they had several options for itineraries to follow. See "Hubbard's Guide to Moosehead Lake and Northern Maine – Annotated Edition (2020)," for additional details on trips in the region.

ANTICIPATION

Chapter II

"A bard is weak enough you'll find,
A humble cat-gut twangler:
But for a man of simple mind
Commend me to an Angler.
He'll fish and fish the whole year round
Devotedly fanatic,
To catch one fish that weighs a pound
And then his joy's ecstatic."

THE DIFFERENT ROUTES THROUGH MAINE. — THE PARTY, GUIDES, — BAGGAGE, – PROVISIONS, — CANOES, – ARMS. — A CAMP APPETITE. — STUDYING GEOGRAPHY. — THE START. — BID ADIEU TO MOOSEHEAD LAKE. — NORTHEAST "CARRY." — WEST BRANCH OF THE PENOBSCOT. – LANDING FOR OUR FIRST CAMP MOUTH OF MOOSEHORN STREAM.

*

ON leaving Moosehead Lake, the seeker for health or recreation in Maine, who desires to study nature in its primeval state, and drink from her fountains the blessings which she can so bountifully bestow, has three routes of a travel before him. These routes are known as the St. John's River, the West Branch of the Penobscot, and the East Branch of the Penobscot trips, and have for their point of departure the Kineo House, Moosehead Lake, where all that is necessary in camp supplies can always be obtained.[4]

The most frequented route, and on account of its ease generally recommended by the guides, is that to the St. John's River, which one reaches by passing north from Moosehead Lake through the West Branch, Chesuncook, Chamberlin, Eagle, and Churchill Lakes to the Allagash River, and thence northeast through Canada, emerging from the woods at Grand Falls, New Brunswick.[5] The second, or the West Branch of the Penobscot trip, passes southeast through Chesuncook to Ripogenus Lake, and follows the West Branch through Pamedomcook and Twin Lakes into the Penobscot River.

The third and most difficult course through this wilderness, is the tour of the East Branch of the Penobscot, which leaves the St. John's route at Chamberlin Lake, and passes south through Telosmis Lake and then east through Telos and Webster Lake and River to the Matagamonsis and Matagamon or Grand Lake into the East Branch, and after tumbling over the most picturesque falls and rapids in the

---

[4] **2020:** With very few passable roads, the connection by steamer from the Kineo House to the top of the lake was the most expedient way to the rivers.

[5] **2020**: This is the route Hubbard describes in, "*Woods and Lakes of Maine*." See 2020 Annotated Edition.

entire State, unites with the West Branch of the Penobscot at Medway.[6]

PICKING A COURSE

---

[6] Still another trip can be made from Churchill Lake through Spider, Echo, and Mansungan Lake and River, to the Aroostook waters coming out in Maine at Caribou. Col. Lyman B. Goff of Pawtucket, R. I., with his guides Kelly and Mansell, surveyed this route last season, cutting a good path on the many "carries" for the easy transportation of canoes, and to him the author is indebted for new and correct drawings of that region which have been added to this map *(Steele's map)*. But the scenery is uninteresting and the difficulties will not compensate one for the labor endured, and woe betide the tourist if the water is low.

To retain my good health, and enjoy for the fifth season the dearly-loved woods and lakes of Maine, the summer of 1879 soon found me again within her fascinations, a willing captive to her charms. We have never failed in the past to impress upon our friends that one companion is sufficient for company in the woods, but this year, the party although it had small beginnings increased in the ratio of the demands of my tastes. As gathered upon the deck of the little steamer "Day Dream" one bright summer morning, while on her way from the Kineo House to the head of Moosehead Lake, we numbered six souls.

Annotated Edition

Moosehead Lake was once home to many steamers. The estimates range from forty to seventy ships operated on the lake at any one time between the 1830s and the early 1900s.

During Steele's time, there were no roads that reached the northern tip of the lake, making the steamers the main mode of transportation to take loggers and tourists to points along the lake. The boats also carried supplies, and at times towed barges up and down the lake.

At a time when many dams were being constructed in the north woods, the steamers carried food, hay, grain, cattle, and the cement needed to supply the workers and support the operations.

The steamers also rafted logs down the lake in what were called, booms, to the mouth of the Kennebec River. From there, the logs traveled to the mill towns downriver.

Steamer trips on the lake have been described by Thoreau in, "The Maine Woods," and Hubbard in, "Woods and Lakes of Maine."

Today the only operating steamboat on the lake is the Katahdin II. In recent years the 115-foot Katahdin, or Kate as she is known, underwent a renovation and now has a steel hull and is powered by a diesel engine. Passengers are now taken on cruises, and the ship may be rented for private engagements.

Some of the Moosehead Lake Steamers:

Day Dream

Fairy of the Lake

Governor Coburn

Katahdin I

Katahdin II

Marguerite

Moosehead

Priscilla

Rebecca

Ripple

Twilight I

THE KATAHDIN

STEELE'S MOOSEHEAD LAKE REGION MAP

Annotated Edition

Steele's map of Moosehead Lake is circa 1880. It is admittedly difficult to read what was a poster size map pasted into his book. Considering how people get lost in the Maine woods in the current day, I would imagine those using such a sparse map, were expert woodsmen or traveled with local guides.

Many of the maps of northern Maine, while improved during the decades of the 1800s, were still vague and had the barest of navigational use once the explorer was off the main waterways; the highways of the time.

Steele's map, while not as detailed as the Moosehead region map compiled by Lucius Lee Hubbard[7], was certainly better than many maps of the day.[8]

I had chosen for my route this year, the East Branch of the Penobscot River, a canoe paddle of almost two hundred miles, as offering in its swift running streams, lovely

---

[7] **2020**: For more on the Hubbard map, see "*Woods and Lakes of Maine – 2020 Annotated Edition,*" Lucius L. Hubbard. Updated by Tommy Carbone.

[8] **2020**: For map comparisons, see "*Hubbard's Guide to Moosehead Lake and Northern Maine – Annotated Edition.*" Lucius L. Hubbard, updated by Tommy Carbone & Frederick T. Wilcox.

waterfalls, and majestic mountains, that excitement and adventure which my love of nature craved.

Very few tourists to Maine select this, *the hardest of routes*, and we found, afterwards, that we were the *first party who had passed down the East Branch of the Penobscot river during the year* 1879.

In addition to the writer, the party was divided as follows: "Quartermaster," photographic artist, and three guides, named respectively Bowley, Weller, and Morris. My friend who is designated as "Quartermaster" did not receive his title from any such position in my expedition, but from holding an office of like character in a New England regiment during our late war, and he proved by the daily use of his knife in arranging the comforts of the camp, that he was to the manor born.

Our artist was from the "Land of Steady Habits," whose sole duty it was to care for the delicate camera and glass plates, together with the necessary but ill-flavored bottles of his kit, and to be constantly on the alert for choice, or grand bits of scenery along the route. In such a tour as this, with the many accidents ever attendant on camp life, it was no small matter to carry through the wilderness the articles pertaining to our photographer's kit.

We had fifty glass plates six by eight inches each, which were prepared and developed on the ground by what is known as the "wet process." Careless treatment in cartage on the "carries," or a sudden jar might at any moment damage them beyond recovery, which would immediately subvert one of the principal objects of the exploration. Then each chemical had its individuality of importance, from the ether to the collodion, the destroying of which would put an end to the pleasures of photographing.

The first and oldest of the guides, Bowley, was a man of forty-eight years, and lived at Shirley, Maine. He was five and a half feet high, weighed one hundred and ninety pounds, had brown whiskers, turning to gray, checkered shirt, weather-beaten suit, soft brown hat, and a kind sympathetic face, which I found before the trip was ended truly expressed his manly character. I was sometimes inclined to think him slow, and to find fault with the consumptive color of his biscuit and "flipjacks," and urged him to greater diligence and variety in the cooking department, but in matters of importance he always proved his soundness — but he had one fault, he could scent a "carry" three days ahead, and remember its hardships and burdens two days after. He delighted to tell of his many interesting experiences in the wilderness, and of his geological researches through Maine some years ago with Prof. Hitchcock, of Amherst college, while his moose, bear, and caribou stories were endless.

The second guide, Weller, aged thirty-seven years, was a French Canadian from Quebec, but living at this time in Greenville, Me. He was five feet four inches high, weighed one hundred and fifty-one pounds, with reddish moustache and whiskers, brown hair, and was dressed in a dark-colored woolen suit. He was a fine waterman, and occasionally witty, as is proverbial with his class.

THE GUIDES

Bowley.   Morris.   Weller.

The third and last guide, Morris, was a vivacious young man of twenty-three summers, but who looked all of thirty. He was about five feet three inches high, weighed one hundred and sixty pounds, had light brown hair and moustache. Dark blue flannel shirt and woolen pants constituted his habiliments, which latter garment early in the day proved its inferiority by sundry tears which gave him a picturesque appearance highly appreciated by our artist.

A black felt hat was the crowning feature of his attire, around which was wound "casts" of varied colored artificial trout flies. He was the most venturesome canoeman of the party, ever first to try the dangers of the many waterfalls and cataracts on our route. Morris was also the hunter, and many a plump duck and partridge found its way to our table through his activity, which quality is always appreciated by the camper-out.

Our personal belongings were numerous, consisting of woolen and rubber blankets, rubber wading stockings, moccasin shoes, fly rods, guns, landing nets, a lantern, and the very necessary black-fly ointment, consisting of oil of tar, glycerine, gum camphor, and oil of pennyroyal. We also had extra changes of underclothing, woolen stockings, buckskin suits, and an assortment of tools, waxed ends, and silk thread for the repairs of broken fly rods if such should be our misfortune.

The number of weapons composing our armory was one Sharps, one Ballard, and one Spencer magazine rifle, one 38-caliber revolver, and a double barrel shot-gun which also contained two auxiliary rifle barrels. Each man also carried the usual long sheath knife, which latter article was never drawn in a more deadly conflict than that between hard tack and salt pork; nevertheless it was often a trial which brought into play the most heroic invincible against the attack of wild beasts, while at the same time it encouraged such hopes of success in the capture of wild animals that it even troubled the nightly rest of some of the members of the expedition. Three birch-bark canoes and one portable folding canvas canoe constituted our ships of burden, which exerted great influence in exploring the wilds, and added to the enjoyment of its pleasures.

How much poetry and romance the words, birch-bark canoe, suggest to our mind !⁹ the grand old forests have more tender associations when one is paddled through their lights and shadows in a birch canoe; there are thoughts and reveries which make themselves felt as one examines their construction — a natural fitness of things to the regions in which they are used.

---

⁹ **2020**: Punctuation mid-sentence seems to have been somewhat common in Steele's writing.

WE DREAM OF GAME

The delicate-colored bark stripped from a prominent tree is cut at the ends and gathered up into uniform bow and stern, cut and then brought together again at the sides alternately to lift the lines fore and aft; this gives a surface to meet the waves, producing that buoyancy so pleasing to the craft.

Then a gunwale, of strips of wood, is affixed, sewed with spruce roots or rattan, and the whole lined from stem to stern with thin strips of wood called "knees." A birch canoe will weigh from eighty-five to one hundred and fifteen pounds when averaging eighteen to twenty feet; but I have occasionally seen those that weighed three times that amount, and had a longitude of twenty-eight to thirty feet.

My portable canvas canoe made for this special occasion was fifteen feet long with a weight of only forty-five pounds, when the fish-rod-like stretcher was inserted. This canoe could be collapsed at a moment's notice, placed in a bag seventeen by thirty-eight inches, and carried on the shoulders with ease by one person, while it would float eight hundred and fifty pounds.

Before the month's journey was completed, I found I could leap falls and rapids more safely than in a birch bark canoe, and although I often paid for my audacity by cutting its surface, it was easily sewed, waterproofed, and I continued my way. On account of its convenient construction and weight it could be easily transported through the woods to the small bodies of water off our main course, and explorations made not accessible to a birch canoe.

As we were to pass through a country uninhabited, we were obliged to provide ourselves from the start with food sufficient for the entire thirty days' sojourn, and it may be interesting to the reader to know the quantity and variety of the supplies, should he ever undertake a similar enterprise. We did not rely upon the game or fish of the country we were canoeing; like excursions in the past had taught us that these articles were more incidental surprises, than an excess of the daily menu.

HOME APPETITE **CAMP APPETITE**

A "camp appetite" is something entirely different from what one enjoys at home. One would turn in aversion from the plainness of the fare were it placed on the table. But the surroundings and the daily vigorous exercise seem to make one forget the homely dishes, and articles refused at our own boards are devoured in the woods with avidity. Most of the provisions were packed into wooden pails of various sizes, the balance in canvas bags, and were assorted as follows: thirty-four pounds of hard tack or bread, seventy three pounds of flour, one bushel of potatoes, twelve pounds of salt pork, four pounds of beans, two packages of baking powders, two and one half pounds of cheese, ten pounds of ham, three pounds of candles, one bottle each of pickles and chow-chow,[10] three cans of potted ham, seven and three-fourths pounds of onions, twelve pounds of canned corned beef, six pounds of maple sugar, one dozen cans of condensed milk, three pounds of tea, seven pounds of coffee, and thirteen pounds of granulated sugar, besides a quart of oil for our lantern, which latter article was one of the most useful of the lot. Sugar, either maple or granulated, always disappears in the woods at an early date, and the immense quantities of luscious blueberries and blackberries to be had at any time along our route greatly facilitated its departure.

Our canoes, when packed with all the above articles, and further embellished by sundry tea and coffee pots, kettles, frying-pans, broilers, bakers, tin plates and cups, reminded one of the early days of our forefathers and their pilgrimages to the "far west." The country towards which we had set our faces was entirely new to tourists, and but one of our guides (Weller) had ever explored its hidden depths, and even his

---

[10] **2020**: A relish or pickled vegetable condiment.

memory was so treacherous as to be of little service to us. Recently issued maps were faulty, and we were obliged to make many corrections on them and manufacture the geography as we sailed along.

On reaching the head of Moosehead Lake our many boxes and bags, just enumerated, were transferred to the sadly dilapidated wharf at the Northeast "carry," and afterwards removed by the guides to a heavy lumber-box wagon drawn by a single horse, while the birch canoes, supported by long poles, were lashed at the sides of the cart.

MORRIS'S NORTHEAST CARRY

Our artist, to secure his photographic materials against harm, rode in front with the driver, but the writer, in company with the quartermaster and the guides, trudged along in the sand at the rear.

This "carry" or path is about two miles long, rising gradually towards the middle from each end, and terminates on the north at the West Branch of the Penobscot River. There are log houses where one can obtain dinner at either end of this portage, but as our guide, Morris, lived at the further point, our party chose to lunch at his house, and our recollections of his mother's preserved strawberries, fresh cream and bread are alive to this hour. After dinner we immediately betook ourselves to the river's bank, launched the birch canoes, stretched the canvas canoe into shape, and, balancing the crafts to a nicety with our baggage, swung off down the stream for a month's exploration of the inmost heart of Maine.

One well knows the delights attending a picnic in the woods for a day — arising at early morn and carefully stowing away in baskets sundry choice and toothsome articles, and filling the corners of the basket with beautiful bright flowers from our gardens, we resorted to the woods and dividing into groups under the shady trees we spread on temporary tables the savory dishes, and strove to the best of our ability to get in sympathy with nature.[11] But think of a month's picnic *daily* filled with excitement and pleasure,

---

[11] If I ever write another book, I think I shall eschew sentiment. I thought at the time that "sympathy with nature" was very good, but I find that it has been thrown away on at least one — the artist. T. S. S.

from running rapids and falls in a canoe to enticing the wary trout, or picking strange flowers and berries by the brookside, and at night resting one's tired but invigorated body under a snow white tent!

The West Branch of the Penobscot (or Rocky) River, after leaving the terminus of the Northeast "carry" at Morris's, flows steadily to the southeast with hardly a ripple for some two miles until it reaches the mouth of Lobster Stream; then a stronger current is perceptible with "rips," and this continues for two and a half miles more, when after passing a small island the water again becomes "dead."[12] The birch barks, paddled by guides Weller and Morris, preceded us down the river, while the quartermaster and I followed in the canvas canoe, the fourth canoe with Guide Bowley and the artist bringing up the rear.

Could there have been a looker-on from the shore, he would possibly have thought it was a government expedition in search of the "northeast passage;" but although our destination was about as little frequented it was not so grave an affair.

After paddling until late in the afternoon through eight or ten miles of still water we made our first camp on the right bank of the river, at the mouth of Moosehorn Stream, and

---

[12] **2020**: Dead-water is the term used for slow meandering water with little current.

transferring our "kit" to the shore turned over our canoes in the sun to dry.

IN SYMPATHY WITH NATURE

Annotated Edition

Lobster Stream, depending on the height of the water in Lobster Lake sometimes flows into the Penobscot, and at other times flows into to the lake. In either case, this is one of the prettiest streams to paddle and the current is not strong in either case, other than early in the spring, or after heavy rains. Paddling on the stream towards the lake will afford one a view of both Lobster Mountain and Katahdin.

LOBSTER MOUNTAIN – FROM LOBSTER STREAM

The trip over the roads to the put-in on Lobster Stream is rough going on the unpaved Golden Road. The traveler is advised to be prepared with necessary overnight emergency supplies as well as spare tires. If only there were steamer trips from Greenville to Northeast Carry running today, it might be an easier way to reach Lobster Lake over the "carry" than by vehicle on the roadway.

DISCOURAGEMENTS

"CHANGING PASTURE"

Chapter III

"Within the sun-lit forest,
  Our roof the bright blue sky,
Where streamlets flow, and wild flowers blow,
  We lift our hearts on high."

OUR FIRST CAMP AT MOUTH OF MOOSEHORN STREAM. — ACCOMMODATING ONE'S SELF TO CIRCUMSTANCES. — THE "RIPS" OF THE WEST BRANCH. — RUNNING THE RAPIDS. — PINE STREAM FALLS. — CHESUNCOOK LAKE. — UMBAZOOKSUS RIVER. — A "BEAR" WELCOME. — MUD POND AND "CARRY." — A PICTURE DIFFICULT TO PHOTOGRAPH. — THIRD CAMP ON CHAMBERLIN LAKE.

*

A description of our first camp in the woods will acquaint the reader with the arrangement of the many after, and make him familiar with the picture of our daily surroundings.

Our wall tent, ten by twelve feet, was soon unfolded, and, selecting a prominent point of the high bank which commanded the river, we immediately set about cutting the three necessary poles on which to erect it. We trimmed all projecting twigs from the ridge and front upright poles, but left them on the rear one that we might make it useful — on which to hang cups, belts, candlesticks, and lantern. Here the quartermaster's whittling propensity came in use, and another pole was notched by him and pressed into service beside the last, which served as a rack for our guns and rods. Great care was taken that the notches which held the ridge pole were not too long, or they would tear the tent, and that the angle of the roof should accommodate any passing shower. Then we cut short pins from the white birches, and with the ropes at the sides soon drew the tent into position.

PENKNIFE SOUVENIRS

While Bowley, our cook, was making bread and coffee, frying salt pork and trout for our evening repast, the resounding blows of Weller's axe could be heard in the forest, gathering logs for the campfire, and Morris was cutting fir boughs for the historic camp bed. It is wonderful how comfortable a bed this makes, while its delightful health-giving odor is so invigorating to the system. Our table outside the tent was usually made of four forked sticks on which we put others crosswise, and on these we laid splits of wood, and for seats rolled into position a convenient log, or used the many wooden pails containing our provisions. On rainy days we sat on the ground in the tent, and used these pails of various sizes and heights as our "extension table," smiling to think how easily we could conform to any condition in the woods. At the head of the tent a choice position was given to our photographer's camera and chemicals, together with our traveling-bags, rifles, cartridge-boxes, and books, while at our feet were distributed the pails of provisions, and heavier part of our "kit." About one and a half feet was allowed to each man for sleeping accommodations, an imaginary line only dividing off the guides, we being arranged somewhat similar to sardines in a box, only our heads were all in one direction.

Immediately after leaving camp the next morning we entered the "rips" or rough water of the river. For about ten miles there was little necessity of paddling, the velocity of the stream sweeping us along without extra effort. These last few miles were very exciting, as, following in the wake of the birch canoes, we guided our canvas craft past boulders and sunken rocks, while the guides, constantly on the alert for our welfare, shouted or waved their hands to warn us of dangerous places. Passing close to the bank on the left of the boisterous water, we shot the Pine Stream Falls[13] and soon rested in the foamy waters below, where our artist at once immortalized the party.

PINE STREAM FALLS

---

[13] **2020**: Hubbard, in, "Hubbard's Guide to Moosehead Lake," provides the itinerary duration for this and other trips in the Moosehead Lake region. See 2020 Annotated Release edition.

The amount of strength and activity displayed by the guides in handling their canoes past falls and rapids is astonishing. With their slender "setting poles," eleven feet in length, armed at one end with a sharp iron spike of six inches, they will steer the canoe with unerring certainty, or hold it quivering in waters that would seem to engulf it.

A hasty lunch, and we soon reached the mouth of the West Branch (eighteen miles from the Northeast Carry), where a scene of special beauty burst upon us in the white capped waves of Chesuncook Lake and distant view of Mt. Katahdin and the Sourdnahunk range. Paddling across the head of Chesuncook Lake, which is seventeen miles in length and three miles in width, we passed the mouth of the Caucomgomoc Stream and entered the Umbazooksus River. We had hardly recovered from the exertion in crossing the lake, when we espied in the tall meadow grass on the bank of the stream a large black bear, who, standing on his hind legs, nodded an approving welcome. The quickness with which he dropped on his four feet and plunged into the thicket gave us little opportunity to return the compliment with our rifles.

MUD POND CARRY

Another camp, and the next day we passed in safety the Umbazooksus Stream and lake, and at 8 A.M. arrived at the long-dreaded Mud Pond "carry." This path through the woods to Mud Pond is a little over two miles long, and is detested by tourists and execrated by the guides. Many weeks

before my departure for Maine, I had been accosted by a
friend (who had made the St. John's trip), and asked to give
him on my return the full particulars of my experience on this
"carry." I was not, therefore, taken by surprise, but was
prepared to meet it manfully on its own ground, and fight the
battle to the best of my ability. I had provided myself for this
special undertaking with long rubber wading pants or
stockings, reaching to my hips, and further incased my feet
in a heavy pair of canvas hob-nailed shoes, the latter I also
found useful in wading streams. Even while selecting our
provisions at the Kineo House, this and that luxury had been
debated upon, or withdrawn as an article too heavy for
transportation on Mud Pond "carry." Its obstacles to our
senses had also been made prominent by the daily
conversation of the guides, and our imagination of that "gulf"
greatly awakened. On reaching the portage, the canoes were
drawn ashore, turned over to dry, goods removed, and, each
one selecting what he could support, we started off "Indian
file" to make the best of the difficulties. On the right-hand
side of the path, within a few rods of the Umbazooksus Lake,
will be found a cool and refreshing spring of water, at which
we quenched our thirst. At first the path was dry, and only
occasional pools of water, easily turned, interrupted our
advance; but soon the pools grew thicker and thicker,
lengthening to greater extent than before, and, with our loads
on our backs, we plunged forward, sinking time and time

again to our knees in the soft muddy water. It makes a vast deal of difference, the nature and position of the load on one's back, and whether it is steady in its place, or has a shifting propensity. I have known a pair of oars dodging about on one's shoulders to be heavier and more inconvenient than five times that burden in guns and ammunition. I had selected as the task for my left shoulder my shot gun, and attaching to it a broiler, coffee-pot, gridiron, and other impedimenta of camp and cooking utensils, detailed to the right a bag of two hundred shot and rifle cartridges. Picture not only one but six men so loaded, forcing their way through the muddy path, slipping and floundering, first on one side and then on the other, under the conglomerated load of "camp kit." An opening in the dark hot woods halfway across, and our burdens are lowered to the ground, to return to the lake for another cargo. A lunch, and on we go another mile, where the branches lock closer and closer about us, making our load seem double its weight, until with joy we discover from a slight elevation at the end of the "carry" the tranquil surface of Mud Pond. A portion of this course is evidently at some seasons of the year the bed of a brook, and the writer found in a small isolated pool of water only a foot square, a lively trout, four inches in length.

Our guides told how, during some months of the year, they had dragged their boats two-thirds of the way across, remarking that the only "dry" part *this* year, was the temperate way in which they were treated.[14] The canoes on the guides' shoulders were the last loads to cross, and, as it was now 6 P.M., one can make some estimate of the work done, seeing we had only accomplished two miles that day.

---

[14] The use of ardent spirits in the woods ought never to be allowed by either sportsmen or guides. There is enough stimulant and health in the pure air, the piney woods, and clear cold water of the streams, to satisfy any one, while the indulgence often places the sportsman's life in jeopardy. The awkward turn of the paddle in swift water, or the careless handling of a gun by your partially intoxicated guide, may at any moment bring disaster to your canoe or death to yourself, while the selection of a guide should *always* be a matter of the greatest importance, as he has the faculty of making your camp life happy or miserable. A friend of the author started to camp in the Adirondacks sometime since, but discovering in his guide's "kit" a bottle of liquor, and, being unable to obtain the refusal of its use, took the fellow a three days' tramp back to the settlement, and hired another guide, rather than take his chances with the first one. Scientific analysis has long since exploded the *health giving properties* of ardent spirits, and in Arctic explorations the line has been drawn between the vitality of men who drank water or coffee. As regards using stimulants in the woods, I say in the language of Mark Twain — "don't! DON'T!! **DON'T** !!!"

2020: In his books, written roughly of the same period, Hubbard made similar comments to those of Steele's above regarding alcohol use in the woods. This may have been solely for the purposes of safety, or it could have been a more general sentiment of the times. Maine first enacted laws prohibiting the manufacture and sale of liquor in 1851.

Annotated Edition

With all the dams that were devised, canals channeled, and even railways raised, to transport logs in the north woods, the distance of Mud Pond Carry was never valuable enough real estate in the venture of logging to consider flooding. Thus, Mud Pond Carry is in the exact same shape at the time of this writing, as it was in 1880. Descriptions of recent travels on internet blogs are full of accounts of the pains in crossing this mud path. If it was not, the experience would not be the same as relayed by Thoreau, Hubbard, Steele, and many other early explorers and sportsmen.

**MUD POND
LOOKING EAST FROM END OF CARRY.**

Launching our canoes on Mud Pond, some two miles in width, of uninteresting scenery, we bent our remaining energies to the reciprocating paddle, and were soon on the other side, and canoeing the sluggish waters of Mud Pond Stream. Its mouth was clogged by great weather-beaten logs, which necessitated the laborious use of our axes before forcing a passage into Chamberlin Lake. The sun was hardly half an hour above the horizon, as we crossed this beautiful lake two and a half miles to the opposite shore, and camped on its white pebbly beach at the foot of a farm. This was the only one of three habitations which we saw on our trip, and the delight which we experienced was as great as the recovery of a lost trail in the woods by the tourist mentioned in the following incident. A brother angler, while treading a lonesome path in this very neighborhood, found one day a piece of birch bark nailed to a tree on which was inscribed these familiar lines –

"This is the way I long have sought

And mourned because I found it not."

AN ANGLER'S MESSAGE

REFLECTIONS

Chapter IV

"On the fair face of Nature let us muse,
And dream by lapsing streams and drooping wood;
Tread the dark forests whose primeval ranks
Since the Creation dawn have cast their shade."

*

CHAMBERLIN FARM AND LAKE. — A NOVEL FLY
TRAP. — A LESSON IN NATURAL HISTORY. —
TELOSMIS LAKE. — THE "CUT." — A THREE DAYS'
RAIN STORM. — WEBSTER LAKE AND DAM. — AN
APPARITION. — THE WEIRD STILLNESS OF THE
PRIMEVAL FORESTS. —AN ACCOMMODATING
FLY-CATCHER.

*

CHAMBERLIN FARM consists of one log house, eight or
ten barns, and about three hundred acres of cleared land, if
where in some portions you can jump from stump to stump
can be called "cleared land."

The buildings are situated on a hill fronting the lake, and
command a view of the greater part of the water. Mr. Nutting
(who with his three sons has charge of the farm) is six feet
high, straight as an Indian, with heavy high cheek bones,
black moustache, and whose face is thoroughly tanned by
exposure to the sun. The farm, with others in this vicinity, is

owned by Messrs. Coe & Pingree of Bangor, Maine, who possess vast tracts of this wilderness, which they lumber and pass the result of their efforts to the markets along the coast of the State.

Annotated Edition

While E. S. Coe was a successful businessman in Maine, he had started out working for David Pingree, and was only a part owner in Chamberlain Farm when Steele visited.

David Pingree was a Salem, Massachusetts shipping merchant who began purchasing significant tracts of Maine timberland as early as 1841. His holdings far outweighed Coe's, and included Katahdin Iron Works.

E. S. Coe was an engineer and proved himself several times in selecting lands for Pingree; two of the most noteworthy were the Telos Canal and Chamberlain Farm.

In 1844, Coe advised Pingree to buy land around Chamberlain Lake. Pingree subsequently purchased several townships around Chamberlain and Eagle Lakes, and it was on these lands where Coe selected the location for the farm.

The land for the remote Chamberlain Farm grew to over 600 acres, the largest of the farms in the region. The location was far from the typical logging routes and was only accessible in summer by boat and in winter over the ice or packed snow.

Coe was placed in charge of managing the farm and logging operations that it supplied. The land that Coe selected for the farm was strategic to the Pingree operation between the Chamberlain Dam and the Telos Dam. It was well suited for crops, animals, and a supply of fresh water.

By 1858, Pingree had sold Coe a nine-fortieths share of the farm. By the mid-1800s Coe had purchased, through his own means, several townships in the Allagash region.

Over the course of a half-century, the Pingree and Coe partnership had acquired over a million acres of land between them. Coe died in 1899.

A fascinating history of E. S. Coe can be found in Dean Bennett's 2002 article.

*Bennett, Dean B.. "E. S. Coe and the Allagash Wildlands." Maine History 41, 2 (2002): 90-116. (*Available from digital-commons online.)

**CHAMBERLAIN FARM AND LAKE –
LOOKING WEST.**

During the summer months the products of the farm are gathered into the barns, and are used to feed the hundreds of "log drivers" who in the winter and spring are annually sent to this region. These " loggers" are a hardy set of men, receiving a dollar and a half a day when "on the drive," and work from 2 A.M. to 10 P.M., often exposed to great perils and the inclemency of the weather. Large herds of cattle and sheep are pastured here, and on the hill at the rear of the house I noticed a number of mules.

THE ROOM INTO WHICH WE WERE USHERED

The two-story log house in which resides Mr. Nutting is painted an Indian red, and has the only embellishment of any of the buildings. The interior is white washed, and has three rooms on a floor. The room into which our party was ushered had low ceilings of heavy logs, blackened by age and smoke from the big square iron stove which held undisputable possession of the center of the apartment. In one corner was a great box containing wood, which also served as a bed when other accommodations were not available. From the ceiling, hardly seven feet high, was arranged the clothes line, on which hung a portion of the week's washing, while the floor was made of logs with enough openings between them to admit plenty of fresh air. Artistic taste had not been wanting in the decoration of the log walls, and engravings cut from illustrated papers were tacked thereon, while in a prominent position was hung the portrait of a late unsuccessful candidate to presidential honors. Rough shelves nailed to the sides of the walls between two windows supported a roll of old papers, a Webster's dictionary, National fifth reader, Greenleaf's arithmetic, a Bible, and Testament, while at their side hung a mirror, and the family hair-brush and comb. But the most novel article in the room was a fly-trap, which, although it displayed the inventive genius of the locality, can hardly have its model on the many shelves of the Patent office.

This fly-trap hung from the ceiling near the stove, and was manufactured from two shingles fastened together at the butts like an inverted V. On the inside was spread molasses, and as fast as the insects became interested in its sweets, it was the duty of the passer-by to slap the boards together and destroy their contents. In addition to superintending this farm and stock, it is the duty of Mr. Nutting to provide for the various logging camps in the neighborhood, and to watch for the first indication of fires, whose destructive power in the pine forests he fully realizes.

NOT FOUND AT THE PATENT OFFICE
(an early homemade fly-trap)

CAMP ON CHAMBERLAIN LAKE

Chamberlin Lake, on which we had pitched our tent, is fifteen miles long and three miles wide. It has an area of twenty square miles, is 1,134 feet above tide water, contains a number of islands, and took its name from an unfortunate man lost some years since on its shores. Years ago a large dam was built at its northern outlet into Eagle Lake, and the water driven back south, through an artificial cut between Telos and Webster Lakes, thus enabling the lumberman to "drive" his logs to a home market through the East Branch of the Penobscot river, instead of by the St. Johns route to the foreign one of New Brunswick. It costs fifty dollars a ton to transport supplies to this farm, and flour is nineteen dollars a barrel.

After our labors on Mud Pond "carry," we rested here three days, taking photographs of the scenery, and making excursions to the dams between Chamberlin and Eagle Lakes, where we found plenty of exercise for our trout rods. We also "sacked" our canvas canoe across the hills on the east to Indian Pond in search of wild ducks and trout, but were only rewarded by a study in natural history which seldom happens to the forest lover. Our discovery was a family of loons, or the great Northern Diver, a bird the size of a goose, and the finest on inland northern waters. It could be honestly said, "they lived in flats," as their rough nest, composed of sticks and moss a foot in height and two feet in width, rested on a flat sandy knoll which stretched out into the water. Against the unmistakable dislike of the parent birds, I paddled to the front door of their house, and, gazing in, discovered a recently hatched bird and one egg.

A STUDY IN NATURAL HISTORY

The egg was dark brown, spotted with black, eight and seven-eighth inches at the longest, and seven and one quarter at the shortest circumference. The young bird had every appearance of a goslin,[15] with down of a grayish black, and did not seem in the least annoyed as I stroked its glossy coat. Withdrawing my canoe, and creeping quietly back into the thicket, I enjoyed the lesson in frog catching, taught the young one by the old birds, and I left them undisturbed in their happiness.

It was with great reluctance that we broke camp early on the morning of August 12th, rolled our tent, and, arranging our kit in the canoe, paddled out into Chamberlin Lake and bade farewell to the scenes around which clustered so many pleasant memories.

The fresh milk, butter, and eggs of the farm were a happy relief to our regular fare of salt pork and hard tack, while the fresh straw, which Mr. Nutting so kindly offered us from his barns, for the floor of our tent, added greatly to our comfort.

But we had not started with the idea that in this wilderness we were to enjoy all the *dainties* of life, for in order to explore its depths we must give up luxuries and comforts which at home seem indispensable.

How often in my earlier years, while pursuing the study of geography at school, did my pencil in drawing maps wander over this endless tract of territory to the north and east of Moosehead Lake, striving to picture to my imagination its elements.

---

[15] **2020**: Gosling - a young goose. Newly hatched loons have downy feathers.

This great lake near the center of the State, together with few of the largest rivers whose source then seemed a doubt, were about all that relieved the picture, and I was daily discovering new beauties of scenery little known to the outside world.

> *"A land of streams! Some, like a downward smoke,*
>
> *Slow-dropping veils of thinnest lawn, did go;*
>
> *And some through wavering lights and shadows broke,*
>
> *Rolling a slumbrous sheet of foam below."*

Through the long stretches of deep water of Chamberlin Lake we paddled, keeping time with our oars, while on our right arose the peaks of the lovely Sourdnahunk Mountains, each individualized by the bright rays of the morning sun.

Entering Telosmis Lake, which is about a mile in extent, we sailed swiftly through its quiet waters and passed into Telos Lake, where, at the mouth of a brook on the right hand, we were successful in landing a fine lot of trout which averaged over a pound each.

Telos Lake is four miles long and about half a mile wide, and is nine hundred and fourteen feet above tide water, its northern shore rocky and abrupt, in comparison with the sandy and uninteresting nature of its south coast. The mouth of the canal or "cut" at its foot is clogged with immense quantities of flood-wood, old logs, and stumps, bleached to whiteness by the action of the weather, which give it a weird and ghostly appearance against the background of verdure. This "cut" was dug by lumbermen some forty years ago, to pass their logs into the East Branch of the Penobscot, but below the old dam, quarter of a mile distant, one would never suspect by its natural and picturesque shore it was the work of men's hands, the force of water having relieved its sharp outlines.

TELOS CUT AND LAKE

THE WET AND DRY PROCESS OF
PHOTOGRAPHY
AS ILLUSTRATED BY CAMP LIFE

While our artist was preparing his camera for a photograph of the "cut" and lake, our guides "sacked" their burdens and canoes across the *chevaux-de-frise*[16] of old stumps into the "cut," and we pitched our fourth camp on the high bank to the right of the old Telos dam.

Although we had been out fourteen days, we had so far been very fortunate regarding the weather, but we here experienced the first rain-storm of the trip — a genuine northeaster of three days' duration. We had hardly raised our tent and got our "kit" under cover before the watery contents of the heavens began to descend, and we took extra precautions to make ourselves comfortable and endure the trial in the most cheerful spirit possible. But I will not detain the reader with every item of the three days' imprisonment. Encased in our waterproofs, we resorted to the dam, caught trout, or wandered beside the waters of Telos Stream for ducks and partridges, giving little heed to the elements.

It is amazing how little one makes of discomforts in the woods, provided he sympathizes with his surroundings. But to a nature having neither poetry nor romance, to whom a fall is only a suggestion of water power, and a tree so many feet of lumber, the situation is unendurable.

Here our canvas boat was overhauled, cuts sewed and waterproofed, birch canoes pitched, buttons adjusted to our clothing, socks darned, guns and rifles cleaned, while the "Quartermaster" busied himself ingeniously carving pliers,

---

[16] **2020**: A reference to the military defense method of using a frame made of logs with projecting iron or wooden spikes.

scissors, and vises from wood, cutting the joints of the same piece as souvenirs of the locality.

But the storm had one good effect; it nearly exhausted the moose and bear stories of the guides, and left them, in the future, only the current topics of the day to discuss.

TELOS DAM AND RIVER

(Note: notice the wooden cribwork of the dam that would be raised and lowered to control the flow)

So far, the days had been exceedingly warm, — thermometer sixty to seventy in the shade, — but what was our surprise on arising early on the clear bright day of August 16th to discover a heavy frost, and the ice in our camp pails an eighth of an inch in thickness. We were first aware of the event by the exclamations of our cook, Bowley, who was slipping about on the frozen ground outside, and to our incredulous replies, lifted into the door of the tent one of the frozen pails by the tin dipper which adhered to its surface. The tent was quickly "struck" and dried, and, rolling into our rubber blankets and bags our effects, we were cutting the waters of Telos stream, and soon emerged into tranquil Webster Lake at its foot. The brook is about a mile long, and very shallow, and but for the late rain would hardly have been navigable. An easy "carry" of a mile can be found through the tall grass and woods on the right-hand side, which also terminates at the head of the lake.

It is very essential to one's happiness, in making this tour, to know on which side of the stream is the best portage around a fall or rapids, for the knowledge saves many a laborious walk when one's shoulders are loaded.

Webster Lake is a charming little sheet of water about three miles long, and perhaps half as wide, which is wooded down to its very edge. At its foot is another of those series of loggers' dams, about twelve feet high, and on the extreme high bank to the right we again pitched our tent.

Great care had to be taken with our fires along the road, that not a remnant of them be allowed to remain, and the indications are often very delusive. Many years ago, a fire started in the woods on Eagle Lake, and the devouring flames, sweeping southward over fifty miles to this section, destroyed this dam which has since been rebuilt.

There are many decayed and deceptive logs about these old dams, some even a foot in diameter, which at a slight pressure will crumble and plunge one into the deep water below — I speak from experience.

A bear story is always welcomed in camp, not only on account of the truthfulness attending the *first* one, but the doubts which hover around the succeeding tales, add to their interest.

We stretched the canvas of our tent at this place, and while each one was engaged in his various duties, Weller, the guide, pail in hand, sallied out for fresh spring water. He had hardly disappeared from our sight, when with immense jumps he came tearing back through the bushes shouting, "A bear! A bear!"

A rush for our rifles, and a forward movement into the woods. But after an unsuccessful tramp, the she bear and two cubs seen by our friend could not be found.

Before we left the wilderness, we had the unspeakable pleasure of making the acquaintance of some six bears; but on every occasion we were without our rifles, and when we made an effort to hunt them, they were not to be found. We were either shooting a quick flowing stream, and with difficulty keeping our canoes from the rocks, or surprised by meeting them (as in the above case) nearer to camp than one could expect, when they suddenly appeared.

AN APPARITION

WEBSTER LAKE DAM

A few years since, Maine offered a bounty of ten dollars a head on bears, and the hunting or trapping of them was a lucrative pastime, but since the withdrawal of the premium, hunters have decreased in the same proportion that bears have increased.

As might be expected, around the campfire that night, the recent experience suggested hunter's tales, each having its special locality and party designated, who witnessed the exploits, while the habits, courage, and peculiarities of bruin and other animals were discussed to an unlimited extent.

One of the stories told by Guide, Morris, related to a tame beaver which had grown to be a great household pet of a farmer living in the vicinity of Moosehead Lake. One night a defective faucet filled the farmer's sink and overflowed to the floor of the kitchen, whereupon the beaver, following his natural instincts, cut up the chairs and tables of the room, and building a dam about the fugitive stream saved the habitation from further injury!

We tarried three days at Webster Dam, where we captured the largest trout of the excursion, and feasted on many a fine duck and partridge.

To impress the reader with the idea that our table fare was not so hard as might have been expected, I would state that the items of the daily menu consisted of fried brook trout, boiled potatoes, stewed duck or partridge, hard-tack,[17] "flip-jacks"[18] with maple sugar, coffee, and tea. Fish chowders and

---

[17] **2020**: Hard-tack is a simple, dense, survival bread. And as the name implies, it is hard. It held up well to travel and lasted a long time. On the high seas, sailors often called the ration, "dog biscuits," "molar breakers" or "sheet iron."

[18] **2020**: More often called flap-jacks. A pancake.

game stews were our favorite dishes, all eaten with the seasoning of a hearty appetite.

FLY CATCHERS VERSUS FLY FISHING

At this point we were probably as deep in this wilderness as it was possible to get in the trip.

The most striking feature of the forests is the absence of animal life, and more noticeable in our northern than southern wilds. The stately pines of the South stand from eight to twelve feet apart, and with a span of horses one can almost drive from one end of Florida to the other. In fact, the writer, in the winter of 1875, met a party so equipped, traveling in an open wagon from New Smyrna to Fort Capron, choosing their way by the compass' aid. This open condition of things permits the rank growth of vegetation and animal life, which the close-locked branches of our northern forests prevent. In the latter case, also, the continual sifting of the pine leaves on the ground, and the gloom of the overhanging boughs choke what few shrubs might have an existence.

Only along the rivers, or where the woodsman has failed to spare some tree, dare anything but a courageous blackberry or shrub-maple show itself. You may wander for hours in this stillness without seeing a living creature, unless you look sharply enough to mark the insects which toil in the mosses underfoot, inhabit the bark and decayed wood, or wait for you to rest before settling on you.

But we occasionally entertained strangers of animal life, and in one instance, that of an "angelic" order — at least it had wings, and its mission was helpful. Our artist, while casting his line from the apron of the dam, caught it on a projecting beam, and after vain attempts to withdraw it, was successfully assisted by a little brown fly-catcher,[19] who, swooping down, attempted to carry to its nest the bright-colored artificial trout flies.

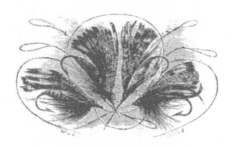

ALLUREMENTS

---

[19] **2020**: Possibly referring to the Great Crested Flycatcher, a common bird of Eastern woodlands.

A STUDY OF TROUT – BY THE AUTHOR

National Academy of Design, N.Y., 1877.

Chapter V

"What time the golden sunset fell,
On wood and stream,
While we, the loss or gain
Recount, and deem
The day all glorious with its rents and stains."

THE PASSAGE OF WEBSTER STREAM. — AN
EXCITING DAY'S SPORT. — THE DAMAGED
CANOES. — THE CANVAS BOAT TRIUMPHANT. —
GRAND FALLS. — PHOTOGRAPHING ALONG THE
ROUTE. — INDIAN CARRY. — EAST BRANCH OF
THE PENOBSCOT. — MATAGAMONSIS LAKE. —
THE DISCOVERY OF A NEW LAKE. — TROUT
BROOK FARM. — GRAND OR MATAGAMON LAKE.
— A CAPTURED SALMON.

AT 5.30 A.M., August 20th, our camp was alive with
preparations for the long-anticipated run-down Webster
River, ten miles, to the East Branch of the Penobscot and, as
it afterwards proved, was the most exciting day's experience
of the two-hundred-mile tour.

Blankets, overcoats, and tent were rolled closer than usual, and leather thongs five feet in length, (some three dozen of which I had brought with me), were tied about them, and safely crowded into the bottom of the long rubber bags. Covers to the various provision boxes and pails were secured with straps and ropes, and every part of the camp kit made to occupy as little room as possible in the four canoes. Rubber leggings and wading shoes were put on, and all unnecessary wearing apparel wrapped in rubber blankets and tied to the boats, that nothing might incommode the free use of our arms in the passage of the falls and cascades of the stream. The stretcher of our canvas boat was fastened to the wooden knees more tightly with thongs, that no possible chance of accident might occur, while the pieces of extra canvas for patching the canoe, with their accompanying needles, wax, and waterproofing, were tied at a convenient place in the bow, and before we had completed the day's adventures we found them of great service.

Webster Stream is about sixty feet wide, and in its course from the lake of the same name to Grand Falls (two miles above its mouth), descends one hundred and ten feet, while the falls, including the rolling dam and cataract below, make the entire distance to the East Branch of the Penobscot not far short of one hundred and seventy feet.

The stream issues from the lake with little force, being clogged above by a mass of logs, the remnants of various "booms." As it passes downward in its course, heavy walls of rock, crowned by tall pines, arise on all sides, often darkening the waters and producing a cañon like appearance of the surroundings.

RUNNING THE RAPIDS ON WEBSTER RIVER

The course of the river is over immense bowlders and ledges, often unobservable, just beneath the surface, while others in sight stand like sentinels in the middle of the stream, disputing one's passage. The flow is repeatedly marked by beautiful falls and rapids, not high, but crowded together in narrow parts, which give greater expression and grandeur to the water, presenting at various points the most remarkable scenery in this section. Cascade succeeds cascade, ending often in an abrupt pitch of three to five feet, and at their base are dark boiling pools, flecked with snowy foam. The river has not great depth of water at any time, three to five feet on the average, but we were fortunate in the extra supply of the last week's rain, which, although it prevented many "carries," also increased the volume and force of water to that extent that made canoeing more hazardous, and filled our path with greater dangers.

The ladened birch canoes had passed us down the river, when the "Quartermaster" and the writer, buckling their belts tighter about them, stepped lightly into the canvas canoe and swung out into the impetuous river, with feelings similar to what might be expected in one entering a battle.

My friend at the stern held a trusty paddle, whose strength had more than once been tried, while the writer, in a devotional attitude on a rubber blanket at the bow, held a long "setting pole" ready for duty at a moment's notice. In half the time I have narrated the above, we were among the furious rapids, battling with their difficulties, and shouting to each other above the roar of the waters, how best to circumvent them. The sun, unfortunately, shone the greater part of the time in our faces, which produced a glimmer on the water, often preventing the discovery of sunken rocks. At one time, while dashing down a cascade, we mounted such a bowlder, and, swinging around, leaped a five-foot fall, stern first, much to our peril. Again, with mighty force we were hurled close to the rocky shore, which only a desperate use of the paddle prevented our striking.

At times we were obliged to hold the canoe in the middle of the stream by the long "setting poles," firmly planted in the bottom, while we made our decision regarding the better of two channels, the dangers of which there was little choice, then on we went through the rush of waters, our "setting poles" keeping time with our eyes, noting the sunken rocks by the water's upheaval, avoiding this sharp ledge, or that rough bowlder, or swinging into the foam of another as we shot swiftly by.

Often with ease we thought to pass a distant rock, but mistaking the velocity of the water, doubled it by a hair's breadth. One fall over which the guides had led their canoes, we amateurs passed in the canvas canoe, the water falling in spray about us, but the cheer for our bravery with which we were greeted at its base, paid us well for the risk incurred.

At "Pine Knoll" we were obliged to let our canoes over the falls by long ropes from the cliffs above, and at another, soon after, two of the guides, Weller and Morris, passed safely in our canvas boat, on account of its slight draft of water, although they carried the birch canoes around. So we continued our rapid progress down the stream, running most of the falls, our boat conforming to each situation, and almost seeming a part of us, and taking an interest in our exploits. At noon we stopped for an hour's rest and lunch on the right bank of the stream, and while disposing of hard tack, canned corned beef, and coffee, our artist plied his profession, and then on we went through other perils.

It was fearfully fascinating, as our four canoes, following each other's lead, dashed onward through dangers which we could hardly anticipate before they were passed, only to be repeated and repeated at every mile of the stream. But the stimulant to one's feelings gave strength and courage and even recklessness, which, in the wild surroundings, made one feel as if no danger was too great to dare. An hour after our tarry for lunch, we entered the deep and narrow chasm of swift, dark water above Grand Falls, and swinging our canoe into an eddy on the left, under the shadows of a great rock (some five hundred feet high), we stepped out on the shore, having completed the excitements of a half-day that many years will fail to erase.

Our canoes had suffered less than we had anticipated. A sharp rock had left its mark on Bowley's birch, which the application of rosin and grease soon rectified. The bottom of the canvas boat had two small cuts about mid ships, so the use of needle and thread became necessary, the "Quartermaster," and *compagnon-du-voyage*, choosing for their *modus operandi* different sides of the canoe, putting the needle back and forth with iron pliers.

LUNCH TIME ON WEBSTER STREAM

IT'S NOT ALL POETRY

A few moments rest, and while the guides were "sacking" the camp kit across "Indian Carry," three-quarters of a mile to the East Branch (at a right angles with Webster Stream), we gathered up the artist's camera and plates, and pushed forward to examine the picturesque beauties of Grand Falls, and catch all we could while the light lasted.

Grand Falls is from forty to fifty feet high, seventy feet wide, surrounded on all sides, for half a mile, by ledges of iron-colored rocks of nearly the same height, which decrease in altitude as they near the Penobscot River below. From a point beneath, the scene is grand in its somber magnificence, as the swift torrent, striking midway upon a projecting ledge in the center of the fall, rebounds in foam flakes, which, after the momentary interruption, continue to fall into the dark whirlpool of water below.

We place the tripod upon a prominent ledge, and, mounting the camera, our artist prepares the plates in his mysterious cloth-covered box or "dark room," while we further exclude the light by covering him with our rubber blankets. But the mist and spray blinds us, and we are obliged to gather up the camera and retreat to another ledge before we can operate.

GRAND FALLS – WEBSTER RIVER

The water, of a dark reddish hue, in strong contrast with the snowy foam, circles around and around in the eddies, kissing the rocks on all sides in its whirl, and, amid the roar of the fall, goes dashing on for about four hundred feet, and then plunges over a "rolling dam" on its course to the Penobscot, making canoeing the balance of the distance on this river impossible.

The light from above, reflecting on the cliff above the fall, glancing with rich beauty on rock and cascade, the fantastic growth of trees on every ledge, make up a fascinating charm that each succeeding picture varies in detail, but which pertains with almost equal force to every part of the entire chasm. While our artist was at work, we busied ourselves gathering the luscious blue and blackberries, and scarlet wintergreen berries which grew in profusion around us; they were of great size, the average blueberry being an inch, and the wintergreen berries an inch and a half in circumference-measurement being taken at the time on the spot.

After filling a three-quart pail with berries, we divided the artist's "kit" among us, found the "carry," and pressed on to camp, to which place our guides had preceded us with tent and canoes.

Supper ended, we again sought the river's bank, a mile below the falls at a place called "the Arches," where, in the radiance of a gorgeous sunset, we again drank to our fill of this picturesque locality. Words fail to describe the beauties of this scene, with which even the guides, slow to recognize the attractiveness of nature, were enraptured.

"O Nature, how in every charm supreme!
Whose votaries feast on raptures ever new!
O for the voice and fire of seraphim,
To sing thy glories with devotion due!"

Around the big campfire that night, each narrated his individual experience of the day's adventures, and the hairbreadth escapes in running the rapids.

"But," says Bowley, the guide, "you should accompany the lumbermen *'on the drive,'* and see the perils they run while starting a *'jam'* on these rivers. Often the logs are piled one upon another, until it seems as if nothing but an avalanche would start them. But one log is loosened, and then another, and another, and in a moment the whole mass goes sweeping downstream with terrific force, and woe betide the unlucky driver in its path."

From the first of the trip to this moment, the guides had failed to praise the working of the canvas canoe, as it came in competition with their birch barks. But this day's trial proved beyond question its qualities, and wrung from them an acknowledgment they were not slow to utter.

"It was fun to watch you, gentlemen," says Morris, to the Quartermaster and myself, as we sat drying ourselves before the fire, "you came over the 'rips' like a perfect duck. I don't believe you could drown the craft if you tried." While the French Canadian, Weller, taking the pipe from his mouth, ejaculated, "Ma fois! she goes over the falls like a chain over a log!"

STARTING A BOOM

A BOOM

On Thursday, August 21st, we wet our canoes for the first time in the East Branch of the Penobscot River, although from Chamberlin Lake to this point it is strictly a part of the same stream under different names.

The river at this spot is only about fifteen feet wide, very deep, with long meadow grass lapping and fringing its border, and flowing with the rapidity of a mill course, each bubble as it shot by seeming to have an individuality of purpose, which to the writer was very amusing.

Hardly had we dropped into our accustomed positions in the canoes before we were swept away from the bank, past the tall alders, and darted with lightning speed down the river a mile and a half and out on to the placid Matagamonsis Lake. This was one of the loveliest bodies of water on our course, dotted with small islands and far-reaching points of shore, the tall Norway pines[20] forming a wall of beauty on either side.

The lake is about one mile wide and four long, and the spruce-covered tops of Traveler Mountains[21] to the southwest are reflected in its mirror-like surface. From the top of a bold crag at its foot we stopped for a sketch of the

---

[20] **2020**: The red, or Norway pine (Pinus resinosa), is native to North America.

[21] **2020**: The Traveler Mountains were named by the loggers who traveled the river and the mountains appeared to 'travel' with them. The mountains in the range are North Traveler, Traveler, and South Traveler.

lake, and then passed downward through the sluggish stream of three miles which connects it with Matagamon or Grand Lake.

METAGOMSIS LAKE

To the left or east of this stream, and half way between these lakes, is another lake about two miles in extent, which we fail to find noticed on any map we have seen,[22] and lies

---

[22] **2020**: Hubbard's map labels this waterbody as, "Big Logon." With the modern dam, built after their time, at the outlet of Grand Lake, First Lake (Matagamon) and Second Lake are joined. With a zoom in of an online internet map you may find a branch of this lake labeled as, "Big Logon."

in close proximity to "Hay Creek," but is not what is termed in this section "a logan."[23] (See Introduction.)

Half a mile from this lake, the stream passes under a foot bridge, which leads to a farm on Trout Brook Stream, the first loggers' camp since leaving Chamberlin Farm, a distance of over seventy-five miles.

DISCOVERY OF A NEW LAKE

---

[23] **2020**: Lucius Hubbard had spelled this term, 'logon.' It was defined as, "a loggers' term, a derivative of 'lagoon.'" It is meant to mean a shallow arm of a stream or pond, typically where lilies and grasses grow.

This farm, owned by E. S. Coe, Esq., of Bangor, consists of four houses built close together, and eight or ten barns, with about four hundred acres of cleared land, through which flows the swift-running Trout Brook. Half a dozen batteaux lay turned over on the grass, bounteous crops of oats and potatoes were ripening in the fields, while the industrious chicken (evidence of civilization) was picking about the doors.

The house where our party dined was occupied by a man and his wife and one small boy. The rooms to this house were low and smoky, like all the rest we had seen, with the big iron box stove in the center; the only change from the usual wall decoration was perceived in an advertisement of Pinafore opera music, which, pasted beside the other illustrations, made us feel quite homesick.

After dinner at the house, our party bade our new-found friends adieu, and paddled down the Thoroughfare into Grand or Matagamon Lake, which is about one-third longer than Lake Matagamonsis, and went into camp at its foot, on the right bank, near another old dam.

The eastern shore of this lake (the largest body of water on our course since leaving Chamberlin Lake) is not especially attractive to the artist, being low and covered with meadow grass. But the western is decidedly picturesque, being bold and rocky, which, climbing from elevation to elevation, finally culminates in the precipitous and rugged peak of Matagamon Mountain, towering above one's head to the height of six hundred feet, and is almost divested of foliage. We halted but one night on this lake, but were well rewarded by the number and size of the fine trout captured, adding also to our creel a small salmon.

OUR SALMON

MATAGAMON OR GRAND LAKE

Chapter VI

"By viewing nature, Nature's handmaid, art,
Makes mighty things from small beginnings grow.
Thus, fishes first to shipping did impart
Their tail the rudder, and their head the prow."

DANGER OF WANDERING FROM CAMP. — AN
EXPERIENCE ON LAKE SUPERIOR. — THE FALLS
OF THE EAST BRANCH. — STAIR FALLS. —
INCIDENTS OF CAMP LIFE. — AN ENCHANTED
BOWER. — HUNT'S FARM. — AN ARTIST'S CANOE.
— THE ASCENT OF HUNT'S MOUNTAIN. — A
REVERIE. — WHETSTONE FALLS. — DISCOVERY
OF JASPER ON LEDGE FALLS. — DAWN OF
CIVILIZATION. — MATTAWAMKEAG. — THE EAST
BRANCH CANVAS-ED.

I often thought how easily one could stray from camp, and,
if without a compass, be lost in this wilderness. While
hunting on Lake Superior one autumn, some years since, I
endured such an experience, and the bitterness of it has
always remained fresh in my memory. While passing over
the corduroy road of thirteen and a half miles which lies

between the town of Ontonagon, Mich., and the Minnesota copper mines, my attention was allured from the road by the melodious whir-r-r-r, whir-r-r-r of a brace of partridges. Stepping aside into the thicket, I followed as fast as possible the retreating sound, and after a tedious tramp through briers and swamp I finally brought them to bag. In the excitement of the chase, I had given little or no heed to the path, or to the clouds that were fast gathering overhead.

Starting back in the direction I supposed the road, I traveled, it seemed to me, double the distance that would have revealed it, but no familiar path did I find. In fact, I was amazed in discovering that I was back on the same ground on which I had started. There was no reason in the thing, — no reasoning against it. The points of the compass had been as clear in my head as if I saw the needle, but the moment I was back, all seemed to be wrong. The sun, which occasionally revealed itself, shone out of the wrong part of the heavens. I climbed one of the tall trees, but the very stillness of the landscape on which I gazed seemed to mock me.

I was not a novice in woodcraft, and could follow a trail readily. I examined the bark of the trees to see which side was the roughest, and then, singling out a number, judged of the points of the compass by the way the majority leaned, and plunging into the thicket made another and another attempt.

I well knew the danger of losing my self-control, and, sitting down on a log, I covered my face with my hands and waited until I felt calm and self-possessed again. I have no idea how long it was, but when I arose the sun was nearly obliterated by the clouds, which soon began to discharge their contents in sympathy for my ill luck, and to reach my destination I must make all speed.

I immediately struck a "bee line" in the direction which my reveries had designated as the right path, blazing the trees with my hunting-knife as I hastened along. Soon, I espied an opening, and, dashing onward, what was my joy to find the old corduroy road, which never looked more welcome in its life.

From Grand Lake to the junction of the East with the West Branch of the Penobscot[24] it is sixty to seventy-five miles, the river being shut in on all sides by lofty mountains, or heavy belts of grand old forests, through which the swift river tumbles, with only an occasional suggestion of the lumberman's axe.

There are eleven conspicuous falls in this interval, varying from twenty to sixty feet in height, while the charming cascades are too numerous to mention. The abrupt descents bear the names of Stair, Haskell Rock, Grand, Pond Pitch, Hulling Machine, Bowling, Spring Brook Gravel Bed,

---

[24] **2020**: Maine Gazetteer map 51.

Whetstone, Grindstone, Crowfoot, and Ledge Falls, their names, in many cases, suggesting their wild and rugged formation.

The water swept so swiftly through this section that with the exception of the last twenty miles it was hardly necessary to use our paddles, but, keeping an eye to the rocks in our path, we could silently enjoy the many lovely changes constantly opening in the landscape.

But this also was decidedly the hardest part of the entire excursion. At most of these falls, our whole camp equipage, provisions, and canoes had to be "sacked" around the falls from one to two miles, and in many cases, there was hard climbing along the steep, rocky sides of the mountains which followed the river's course, while each one of us carried his portion of the load.

For two and a half miles after leaving Grand Lake one is constantly reminded of the day's experience on Webster Stream by the furious rapids, and we were again obliged to call into action our "setting poles." In a drenching rain, we were twice compelled to land on the shore, take the canvas boat into our laps and sew the cuts in its surface, laughing at the philosophical manner with which we submitted to the circumstance.

Along the river's bank to the west, for many miles, are the lovely Traveler Mountains, whose rambling appearance and daily companionship are fully represented by their name.

Stair Falls the "Quartermaster" and myself ran in our canvas canoe, but the guides, tending their birches as if they were glass, dropped them from step to step by means of ropes.

This fall or cascade is a series of steps or stairs some five in number, each about three feet high and ten feet apart, the best passage being through the channel near the left bank. It is a very choice bit of scenery, and one that any artist would greatly desire to transfer to canvas and work into endless variety of composition. A ten-mile passage of the swift river, and we reached Grand Falls, which, although higher than its namesake on Webster River, being followed immediately by numerous cataracts did not so impress one.

Here we were obliged to make a portage of three fourths of a mile through the dense woods to the foot of the falls, and, in a heavy shower, went into camp on the opposite shore. To the "camper-out" a rainy day in the woods is among the most disagreeable experiences, even under a tight tent, with good company and plenty of amusement. But the difficulties increase by being forced to be out in the. storm, and to leave your canoe at a portage and obliged to carry on your back through mud and mire all your camp effects.

DROPPING CANOES OVER THE FALL

ACCEPTING THE SITUATION

Through the woods you stumble, pressing the wet branches aside, which in their recoil push away your rubber clothing, from which the buttons are fast disappearing and the rents appearing, and whose special protection is sadly deficient, until the repetition of such circumstances as thoroughly drenches you as if you had been without them. The water is dripping from off your hat to your neck and rolling down your back in icy rills. The position of your arms in carrying your "kit" is such as to lead a looker-on to imagine you are striving hard to fill your sleeves with the rain, which you know is a mistake, but there is no help for it. You clutch tightly to your rifle as your pack begins to slip, striving to keep the locks from the rain, while your boots have been innocently occupied in catching every scanty drop which fell from your clothing, and you have every appearance, if not the feeling, of the oft-quoted "drowned rat." You would not have your wife, or other friend, see you at this moment for anything. How they would laugh, and hurl at you many of your pet quotations regarding the "poetry, pleasure, and romance of life in the woods," until you had rather endure another storm than their irony.

Then comes the raising of the wet tent into position, the repeated attempts to start the fire, and the holding of every individual fir branch in the flame to dry before performing the duty of bed.

Two forked sticks with one across are placed before the fire, and on them you hang boots, socks, blankets, and other articles of your belongings, and, while the guides are cleaning your guns, you examine the provision boxes to see if they have escaped the drenching.

It is amusing how stoical and indifferent one grows to these circumstances in the woods, and soon makes but little of them, retaining as serene and unruffled a disposition as if they were of no account, while after a warm supper and a social pipe they pass from memory.

STAIR FALLS

I will not weary the reader by a description of the passage of each fall from day to day on our route, some of which we ran, and past others we "carried," letting the canoes, as before, over the difficulties by long ropes from the cliffs above. After passing Spring Brook and Gravel Bed Falls, we paddled through a mile or two of heavy "rips" and entered some two miles of "dead-water."

On turning a beautiful bend in the river, what was our surprise to observe the rugged growth of pines gradually disappear, and the landscape immediately softened by the introduction of a dense forest of maple, elm, ash, and noble oak trees, whose gnarled trunks pushed themselves far into the stream, their branches overlocking above our heads and forming a canopy that darkened the water.

HULLING MACHINE FALLS

Exclamations of surprise rang from our lips as all the canoes in "Indian file" drifted through this enchanting bower, and we thought to ourselves, if in the quiet dress of summer this is so lovely, what must it be when robed in autumnal foliage.

Passing the mouth of Big and Little Seboois Rivers, we pitched our tent on the left bank of the river near a place known as Hunt's Farm.

The solitary log-house and barn on Hunt's Farm[25] were erected some forty-three years ago, and are located on high ground in a picturesque bend of the Penobscot River.

The house outside is painted red, white-washed inside, with low ceilings similar to the others mentioned. In addition to the cultivation of land near the house, an attempt was made some seasons ago to press into tillage, as a melon patch, the side of an adjacent mountain, but the fruit, as soon as it grew heavy and ripened, snapped its hold on the vines, rolled down the mountain side, and was crushed at its base. As can easily be seen, this elevated farm was not a success, and now only the bright green foliage of a fresh growth of trees is left to tell the melancholy story. Mr. Dunn, who, assisted by three other persons, takes care of the place, showed us many attentions, supplying us with fresh milk and sugar, and other delicacies that had been foreign to our fare at camp for many days.

---

[25] **2020**: Hunt's Farm was started around 1835 by William Hunt as a supply depot for logging operations. It was due south of where the Wassataquiok Stream met with the East Branch of the Penobscot. The westerly mountain here is Hunt Mountain.

THE ARCHES
East Branch of the Penobscot River

The manufacture of birch canoes seemed to be one of the industries of the place, an immense one being then in process of building for the celebrated New York artist, Frederick E. Church, Esq.[26] This canoe was twenty-eight feet long, over

---

[26] **2020:** Steele is referring to Frederic Edwin Church, the American landscape artist. His camp, Rhodora, was still standing in the year 2020 and the property has recently been available as a camp rental.

four feet wide (midships), and when completed would weigh three hundred pounds.

The (aforementioned) artist has recently purchased four hundred acres of land on Milinokett Lake,[27] fifteen miles distant, a tributary to the West Branch of the Penobscot River, one of the prettiest sheets of water in that vicinity. A fine view of Mount Katahdin can be had from this spot, and men were to leave this farm the following day to erect three substantial log camps.

HUNT'S FARM

---

[27] **2020**: Now spelled Millinocket Lake. Maine Gazetteer map 51. Not to be confused with the lake of the same name, Millinocket Lake, forty miles to the north, beyond the norther border of what is now Baxter State Park, map 57.

MOUNT KATAHDIN
Study by F. E. Church

The ascension of Mount Katahdin can with little difficulty be made from Hunt's Farm, where a convenient ride on horseback lands one within two miles of its top. I shall not soon forget the climb of Hunt's Mountain, about twelve hundred feet high, opposite our camp, or the magnificent view from its peak.

With Mr. Dunn as guide, in company with the "Quartermaster," I started to make the ascent on the morning of August 24th. To clamber up the steep side of a mountain in the dense wilderness is an entirely different undertaking from the following of a "bridal path" to the top of Mount Washington. Cutting stout poles seven feet in length, we set off up the mountain side, catching half glimpses of the landscape below, as we swung from tree to tree and rock to rock, which latter had been made extra slippery by a recent shower, and, after two hours of laborious climbing, gained the bare but welcome crags at the top. The first sensation of the prospect from the summit is simply of immensity. The eye sweeps the vast spaces that are bounded only by the haze of distance, overlooking one vast undulating sea of forest trees, which seemed to come rolling in to the mountain's base, with only here and there the glimmer of a lake or stream, and little to break the vision save the farm at our feet, where we could just distinguish the white canvas of our camp. To the left stretch successive ranges of hills and mountains, and at their base could be had momentary glimpses of the windings of the West Branch of the Penobscot, while to our right was its twin brother, the East

Branch, over which we had so recently passed, its misty falls and cascades subdued to a level with the surrounding landscape. These two streams sweep away to the south twenty miles, and unite in unbroken union at Medway, on their way to the sea.

Before me arose the cloud-capped peak of Mount Katahdin, 5,385 feet high, Wasataquoik Mountain, 5,245 feet high, the lofty Traveler and Sourdnahunk Mountains, which, with the exception of the first, are wooded to their summits. Broad seams, or slides, are visible along the surface of old Katahdin, which, with its triple-peaked outline, seemed to look down into the valleys with a fatherly interest, while "the whispering air sent inspiration from the mountain heights."

JUNCTION EAST AND WEST BRANCHES OF THE PENOBSCOT

The thunder clouds had just parted, and a beautiful rainbow arched the heavens, shedding its colors on the glistening outlines of the valley and mountain. Oh, that we might be left alone for hours, to watch the changes of the landscape and hear the secret voice and dread revelations of these magnificent mountains!

There are thoughts, deep and holy, which float through one's mind, as, gazing down upon such a scene, one contrasts the smallness of man with the magnitude of God's works, and in the weird silence contemplates the perishable of this world with "the everlasting hills."

After such a prospect of the East Branch and vicinity, it almost seems as if we ought to bid adieu to this enchanting river of our narrative, but if the future tourist shall desire to make its acquaintance, I would like to guide him safely over four other remarkable falls to his journey's end at Mattawamkeag, thirty-two miles below.

Two miles from Hunt's Farm, we came to what is known as Whetstone Falls, a series of high, picturesque cascades. Here we made a short portage on the right-hand side of the stream, then shot across and down a very steep pitch of the water close to the left bank, and landed a portion of our baggage which we carried to a point below. Then the guides ran the heavier part of the falls, and, after passing the quick boiling water at their foot, rounded to the shore and re-loaded the camp kit which we had "sacked" over the ledges at the river's bank. Then we passed, without accident, Grindstone and Crow Foot Falls, each from ten to twenty feet high, the name of the former being so suggestive by its geological formation that the "Quartermaster" declared that he could honestly see the indentation of the axle. Another camp seven miles from Medway, and in the morning we passed Ledge Falls, which, although the last of the pitches on the East Branch, was none the less interesting.

We passengers, to lighten the canvas, strolled along the shore, gathering bright flowers and curious colored stones, while the guides alone in their canoes ran the cataract, meeting us in the "dead-water" below. These falls are composed of slate of a grayish color, which, after the first steep pitch form into numerous cascades, produced by the sharp ridges of rock, which, extending out into the stream from both shores, decrease in height as they approach the center.

A dark red stone attracted my attention, and I waded into the water to secure it, and on regaining the canoe soon after, threw it into my camp-bag, little dreaming of the value of my prize. On reaching home it was examined by an old and experienced lapidary, and proved to be a *jasper*[28] of exquisite grain and color.

---

[28] **2020**: Cryptocrystalline quartz.

A portion of the stone, as an article of jewelry, in crusted with the magic words "Ledge Falls," is highly prized and now worn as a souvenir by the writer.

**GLIMPSES OF CIVILIZATION
BEGIN TO APPEAR**

The stream now gradually widens, with strong but noiseless flow; the mountains retire, and the banks of the river are for the most part bordered by foot-hills and grassy knolls. Glimpses of civilization begin to dawn as we occasionally pass a log house whose lonesome appearance is only relieved by the happy faces of children at the door. Cornfields wave their tall stems, while broad patches of potatoes (for which Maine is justly celebrated) flourish here surprisingly. It is a sudden change from the forest's depths, after a month's camp life, and seems to urge us towards home more and more rapidly.

We are soon at Medway, the junction of the East and West Branches, (a small town on the left bank of the Penobscot River, of about four hundred inhabitants,) and are speeding faster and faster through the broad river to Mattawamkeag on the European and North American railroad.

We have followed the river in its devious windings, from a width of fifteen to now an expansion of over five hundred feet.

We have felt the mysterious silence of the wilderness at early morn, or as the twilight lessened and the shadows deepened about the camp, only broken by the chirp of the cricket, or the weird and plaintive cry of the loons on the lake.

Our tour has been one of daily excitement, filled from first to last with grand old forests, noble waterfalls, picturesque lakes, and cascades. A region in which an artist might linger many weeks with profit to both eye and brush, while the recuperation to one's health by the outdoor life in the dry atmosphere cannot be overestimated.

Springing ashore, we unjoint our rods, pack up the camera, collapse the canvas canoe, and with hearts full of thanks to the kind Providence which has watched over our two-hundred-mile voyage, we bid adieu to our guides, as we do now to the reader.

NET RESULTS

The following fall, in 1880, Steele and a new set of companions set off on another month-long trip in the Maine north woods.

Read their story in:

Paddle and Portage

The Annotated Edition

by

Maine Author

Tommy Carbone

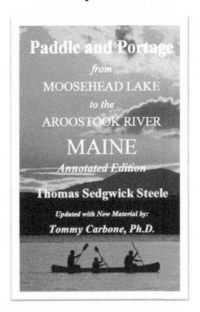

About Tommy Carbone

Tommy Carbone lives in Maine with his wife and two daughters. He studied electrical engineering and earned a Ph.D. in engineering management.

He writes fiction from a one room cabin, on the shores of a lake, that is frozen for almost six months out of the year, and moose outnumber people three to one.

His first novel, "***The Lobster Lake Bandits – Mystery at Moosehead***," has made those 'from away" want to visit Maine. It's a big state – come explore.

*

Books from Maine's

North Woods

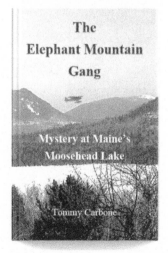

A Maine Novel

The second novel in

the

Moosehead

Mystery

series

Based on the writing of Fannie Hardy Eckstorm this memoir is a wonderful tale of the Maine woods with history from the 1800s.

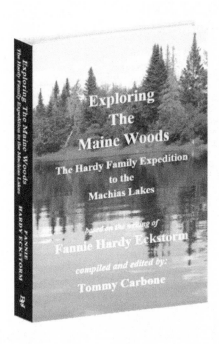

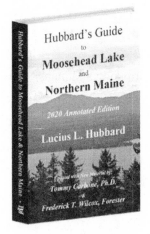

Hubbard's Guide

to exploring

Northern Maine

2020 Edition

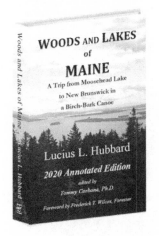

Hubbard's

adventure

through Maine to

Canada.

2020 Edition

The two-book commemorative hardcover edition of
Thomas S. Steele's Maine Adventures.
A great gift for all lovers of the outdoors – or for yourself.

Updated with new information and maps.

Annotated edition by Maine author Tommy Carbone.

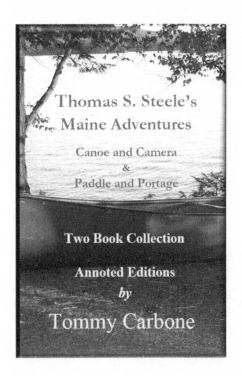

Made in United States
North Haven, CT
04 September 2022

23664489R00093